My Miraculous Healing

My Miraculous Healing

Miracles Performed by God

Sheila P. (Tullos) Johnson

Copyright © 2010 by Sheila P. (Tullos) Johnson.

Library of Congress Control Number: 2010916539
ISBN: Hardcover   978-1-4568-1035-1
             Softcover   978-1-4568-1034-4
             Ebook   978-1-4568-1036-8

All rights reserved. No part of this book may be reproduced or transmitted in any form or by any means, electronic or mechanical, including photocopying, recording, or by any information storage and retrieval system, without permission in writing from the copyright owner.

This book was printed in the United States of America.

To order additional copies of this book, contact:
Xlibris Corporation
1-888-795-4274
www.Xlibris.com
Orders@Xlibris.com

CONTENTS

ACKNOWLEDGEMENTS 11

Introduction 13

-1- "The Test of Faith" 15
-2- "The Practice of Faith" 19
-3- "Faith and Happiness" 24
-4- "A Faithful life in Prosperity" 31
-5- "Faith Regenerated" 36
-6- "Faith in the Resurrection" 42
-7- "Faithfully Encouraged" 46

Dedication

I dedicate this book to my mother Helen Tullos, she was the joy of my life. She had lots of talents; she sang, act, cooked, baked, and much more. She was usually a key character in many of the church plays. My mom was born on March 6, 1925. Her mom died when she was only 5 years old, so she was raised by her uncle and aunt who had plenty of children her age to grow with. She stayed with them until she married and had a family of her own; 5 boys and 2 girls, Henry JR the oldest, followed by Wayne, then there was Charlotte the first girl, then Allen, myself (Sheila), Mike, and Ray the baby boy. Our family didn't have much wealth growing up; we had no running water, no indoor toilet, but we had plenty of love for each other. Mom worked two jobs to make ends meet; when she wasn't at her factory job she cleaned houses. We ate plenty of beans and potatoes, and could always count on those homemade apple and fried peach pies and various type of cakes. Mom, your love kept us all.

We miss seeing your beautiful smile and hearing your soft aged voice.

Helen Fran Tullos March 6, 1925-February 26, 2006
Gone but never will be forgotten

ACKNOWLEDGEMENTS

My Lord and Savior Jesus Christ, you are a healer, provider and much more.

My loving husband Anthony, who stood by my side during the illnesses, I thank you for your support and for your love.

Miranda & A.J., I want to thank you for all your love and support. I am proud to be your mom.

My brothers and sister, who I love deeply, growing up we had much fun together. We have a lot to be thankful for; we thank God for allowing us to have our mother for much of her 80 years.

Pastor Leola McClain, you are a very beautiful and wonderful person. You are like a second momma to me. I thank God for having you as my Pastor and friend for more than 50 years; you are a very strong woman of God.

I would also like to thank my In-laws in Florida and Tennessee for welcoming me in the family.

There are a number of friends who contributed in countless ways and offered prayers in expression of their love for me as I was writing this book. To you I say, "Thank you from the bottom of my heart.

INTRODUCTION

My name is Sheila Paulette (Tullos) Johnson. My parents Henry and Helen Tullos are both deceased. I have five brothers and one sister, I being the fifth child. I was educated through the public school system of Pikeville Tennessee, and there is where I grew with my mom and siblings. At the age of ten I accepted the Lord Jesus Christ into my life. I met Anthony (my husband) in 1982, and was diagnosed with Hodgkin's disease (cancer of the lymph-nodes) later in 1983, but through the skillful treatments of the doctors, and the much needed prayers from my family and friends, but most of all by the Grace and Mercies of God I was healed in 1984.

In June 1984 Anthony and I were married; we were blessed with two children, Miranda and Anthony II (A.J.). In support of my husband's military commitment, the Lord has since allowed us to experience the lifestyle of many European Countries, and visit many cities within the United States.

In 1994, while living in Baumholder, Germany, I worked for two years out of our apartment as a Family Child Care provider (FCC); I kept a multi aged group of children. I loved children and really enjoyed my job, but the greater part of my heart was for the infants. So I later took a Job at the Child development center (CDC), where I was placed in the infant room. Since that initial hiring in Germany of 96, I've worked with CDC in Texas, and Georgia. Training received over those 12 years were in Child Guidance, Fire Safety, HIV, Community CPR, and various USDA Nutritional classes, clearly my prayers were answered.

In 1999, I was diagnosed with breast cancer, but I stood on Gods promise and was healed from the disease. Eleven years later in

2010, I was again diagnosed with breast cancer, but thanks for the Mercy and Power of the Lord God which allows us all to do what we do; I was again healed from the disease. Faithfully speaking, this is my testimony.

-1-
"The Test of Faith"

James 1:2, 3. My brethren, count it all joy when you fall into various trials, knowing that the testing of your faith produces patience.

In 1983, into my 5th year as an employee of Pikeville nursing home, I and other workers were instructed to meet at the front desk, which was a common practice when important information had to be put out. While there the supervisor began to explain that an insurance agent was present and he wanted to talk to us about cancer insurance. The Agent convincingly talked several of us into hastily taking out a policy. About two months after purchasing the policy, I decided that I didn't want it anymore; actually, I didn't like the idea of the extra money coming out of my check. Besides, I really didn't see a need for cancer insurance, I didn't think it would affect me (clearly that was the wrong thing to think).

Three months after cancelling the policy, I noticed that the lymph-node on the right side of my neck was swollen, initially; I didn't think much about it, because the swelling went down. Several weeks later while gazing into the mirror and combing my hair, I notice that the knot had reappeared, that is when I began to worry. I rushed and showed my mom what I had noticed, she sensing my fear and concern, suggested that we go to the emergency room (ER). Once arriving at the ER I was delighted to see that my primary doctor (DR. Quito) was on duty that night, he took a look at me, then admitted me into the hospital for the purpose of a biopsy the next morning. After the biopsy, I am sure DR Quito knew the results were positive for cancer, but he did not reveal it because of his closeness with the family, instead, he told us that he wanted to send me to Erlanger Medical Center for further testing with Dr Nelson.

The following morning my mom and I went to Erlanger in Chattanooga, Tennessee, Dr. Nelson was expecting us, and upon his request, I began to explain my symptoms and concerns; I told him of the night sweats with fevers of 103 degrees, no appetite, a loss of weight and a rash all over my body (it really did itch bad), and I went on to explain that I was always in a state of exhaustion; all I wanted to do was sleep. Dr. Nelson then glanced at the biopsy results, then again looked me in the eyes and told me that I had Hodgkin disease, which was a very frightening moment for me; when the doctor informs you that you have cancer, you automatically assume that you are going to die. My mom and I began to stare at each other, both of us speechless; we did not know how to take this cancer thing, because no one in the family had ever had it. Dr. Nelson then admitted me into the hospital where test after test was ran and all the results came back the same Hodgkin Disease stage two, I tell you, I prayed like I never prayed before, begging the Lord to take this thing (cancer) away. About a week later Dr. Nelson, aided by three or four other doctors came into my room and told my mom and I that my spleen had to be removed, because the cancer had spread into my spleen; this news frighten my mom and I even more, Just imagine, having several doctors to come into your room at the same time, what a scary feeling. I really thought there was nothing the doctors could do for me, so after they told me my surgery date I went to the restroom and prayed that the Lord would do something, quick. As the surgery date and time grew nearer, my mind wondered in and out of faith, and then suddenly the Lord told me to keep the faith, and trust him, because it wasn't my time to die.

The surgery went well, and I was elated to have pulled through, not realizing that it (the surgery) was only one quarter (1/4) of the process; I yet had the bone marrow, which was expected to be very painful, then the chemotherapy and radiation treatment, which is known to be sickening and possibly damaging other cells in the body. After learning all this new information about the post surgery procedures, my faith again began to fail me, but the only thing I knew to do was to constantly pray, not only did I pray, everyone who knew me prayed for my healing, that was very comforting to know that I was loved by so many. Before the bone marrow procedure, I had to deal with the fluid that had developed on my lungs, it was scary, but my mom was there to support me while the doctor and nurses removed it, what a relief afterward.

There were fond memories of my hospitalization after the surgeries; I guess it's a natural instinct, but it seemed as though I grew closer with my doctors, nurses, and other hospital workers, they were very kind and professionals. My mom was there at my side throughout the surgeries and the first week of recovery; I would sometime notice her face as she cringed when I experienced some sort of discomfort, as though she could likewise feel my pain. She daily walked with me up and down the hallway outside of the recovery room, oh what a great feeling to have my momma at my side.

One day my brother (Mike), my sister (Charlotte), and our cousin (Diana) came to visit, we talked and laughed a little, then after a couple of hours my brother was ready to go, and I noticed my mom getting her bags as though she was leaving as well. I began to think to myself "why is she leaving?" and then I realized, my mom was tired, she never would tell me that, but I knew she was tired. Charlotte noticed my expression of sadness, and attempted to comfort me by assuring me that she and Diana was going to stay over-night so that momma could go home and get some rest. I replied O.K, gave my mom a hug and a kiss, and followed her (with my eyes) as she walked across the room and exited the door. Diana left the room shortly afterward vowing to return, when she did I smelled the scent of Kentucky fried chicken as she entered the door, we pigged out on Chicken, mashed potatoes, slaw, and biscuits, what a relief it was to eat something other than hospital food; later that evening Diana surprised me with my favorite dessert, strawberry pie, umm, it was delicious. After dessert, we laugh, talked and walked up and down the hospital hallways like children at play, but a lot slower, and less active. As the evening went on, the night closed with my body in pain, my sister wanted to call the nurse, but I begged her not to, she and Diana couldn't understand why I didn't want anything for the pain, they being unaware that my tolerance for pain had gotten stronger. That day Charlotte and Diana spent with me was really great, though I enjoyed my momma, I really felt that I needed that change of venue, it was truly refreshing.

-2-
"The Practice of Faith"

James 5: 14 *Is anyone among you sick? Let him call for the elders of the church, and let them pray over him, anointing him with oil in the name of the Lord.*

One day my mom and I were in the room watching television, then sister Leola McClain (my Pastor from Pikeville), and brother Shropshire, a pastor from Chattanooga walked in to see me; during their visit a nurse came in with my breathing treatment, I had to blow in this plastic container until the little ball came up to the top, both pastors and my mom were the cheerleaders; they were cheering me on by saying "come on Sheila, you can do it," I had to do this for an hour, so the encouragement was much needed. After the treatment we laughed and talked about the goodness of the Lord for about 2 more hours, the preachers anointed me with oil, prayed, then departed. The day ended just as it started; my mom and I alone reminiscing on the ups, and downs of the day.

A few days later, Pastor McClain returned, this time baring a gift, I gazed closely and recognized that it was a book; she expressed that she wanted me to read it, as she placed the front of the book in my face, exclaiming the title, "God Can Do It Again," by Katherine Kulman. After reading the title I thought to myself, this is going to be some good reading, it was almost as if I couldn't wait to have the pastor pray and leave the room, because I wanted to read that book. While mom dozed to catch a cat nap, as she usually does, I began reading the book, learning of this young woman who like myself, had Hodgkin disease; I read on further about her ordeal and circumstances and how the Lord eventually healed her of the cancer. I was right, the book was good, it opened my eyes more to what faith really was and how to use it as a tool. I immediately got up without disturbing my mom, and hobbled to my secret closet (the bath room), and cautiously, trying not to bust lose any stitches, lowered myself to my knees and cried in a whisper "God you healed this young lady and I know you can and will do the same for me;" that was the day I began putting my faith to work. My understanding of Hebrew 11:1 *(now faith is the substance of things hoped for, the evidence of things not seen)*, is to take hold of a belief and hold on until it becomes reality; from that moment on, every time I prayed, I thanked the Lord God for healing my body, though I was still in much pain, I kept the faith that God would someday heal my body. I found comfort in understanding that God's time was not our time, so that is where faith came in.

Pastor Leola McClain

Just when I thought things were going well, and started to feel really good about my progress, more alarming news was given by my doctor. He and other physicians were concerned that the cancer had gotten into my bones; therefore, more surgery was needed. They had to cut and drill into the top of both my feet; so I was given an option, to either be sedated or just have my feet numbed so that I could watch minor procedure, yes, I chose to watch. The next day I was taken to the Operating Room (OR); they numbed both feet while I watched as they proceeded to make the incision, I felt the pressure of the scraping and picking with the tweezers but I didn't feel any pain (thank God!), they then stitched and wrapped both feet. Afterward I was asked if I could sit up by myself or if I needed assistance from the nurse, I thinking positively, considering what I had just gone through, told them that I could do it myself, I was wrong, as I struggled to left my upper torso, I became light headed and fell back to the bed; at that time with an humble spirit, I welcomed the assistance from the nurse, and kindly accepted a glass of orange juice. The surgery extended my stay in the hospital by one week, it slowed me down but it didn't keep my mom and I from our daily walk down the hallways.

The final week of my stay in the hospital was also the week of my first round of chemotherapy (chemo), oh, it really made me sick; Dr. Nelson had informed my mom and I earlier that if the chemo made me sick he would keep me in the hospital, but he knew that I really wanted to go home, so he let me go. At that time my Uncle Chester and his son Stanly lived in Chattanooga only ten minutes away from the hospital; both opened their homes to us, they didn't want us to make the daily hour and a half drive one way back and forth across the Dayton mountain, my mom accepted the offer, so we stayed three months with Uncle Chester and three months with Stanley and his wife. That was a very good jester and much appreciated, because the chemo made me very sick, and I couldn't imagine having to travel three hours a day, five days a week across that mountain for chemo treatment, oh what a bad experience that would have been. It was bad enough having no appetite, vomiting and losing all my hair; about the only thing I could eat and hold down was water melon, and uncle Chester kept four or five of those around the house. That chemo was so damaging it affected my hand writing, I thought to myself, "I haven't written this bad since I was in a child in kindergarten". Just the thought of having to take chemo the next day made me sick. My mom and I stayed with my uncle and cousin until the full six months of chemo was over.

Prior to the initial round of chemo, I can recall the four weeks of radiation I had to endure, at the time I felt no physical discomfort, not realizing until years later the nerve and cell damage that had occurred in the process of treating the disease. Though I felt no physical pain, I was told by the radiologist that I was burned by the radiation in the chest area; he informed me that the burned area would clear up in about 2 weeks. Again, I found myself on that bathroom floor (my secret closet), praying "Lord I know you are a healer and it doesn't take two weeks for you to do anything, let your healing virtue flow," in less than a week the damage area was cleared, yes, healed by God.

At the conclusion of the radiation, and chemo treatments, my mom and I went back home to Pikeville. It was great sleeping in my bed, walking through my mom house, and going to my church. During every church service, week after week, I would stand and testify of the goodness of Jesus, and thank him for the healing of my body; even when I was in pain from the top of my head to the sole of my feet, my bones ached worst than a toothache, but I worshiped God anyhow. Old Satan really tried to ride me; as soon as I sat down after testifying, that devil would bring to my mind "why did you testify of being healed, when you are still hurting?" I just closed my eyes and called him a liar and demanded that he leave my head, because I'm trusting the Lord, and I know he is going to heal me, I don't know when, but I know that he is, and I am going to stand on it until it became a reality.

-3-
"Faith and Happiness"

Psalm 37:4 *Delight yourself also in the Lord and He shell give you the desires of your heart.*

My cousin Annette, who lived in Bakewell with her husband and son, asked me to go to church with her one Sunday; when they came to pick me up she told me that she had someone for me to meet after church. I enjoyed the church service, and afterward I was rushed to the rear of the church by Annett, then out the door, not stopping to greet anyone (greeting is the customary way of doing things); we stopped outside next to a small group of people conversing, I figured one of them was this person she wanted me to meet. Annett caught the attention of an erect standing young man; he turned toward us and smiled, greeting Annett, Annett then turned to me and introduced me as her cousin Sheila, the soldierly looking man nodded then introduced himself to me as Anthony, that day in April of 1982, I'll never forget. Anthony was stationed in Columbus Georgia with the U.S. Army, but he came to Tennessee every weekend to visit; in November he was transferred to Germany, he wrote me weekly, sending poems, and gifts (how romantic).

Anthony and I became engaged in September 1983, and married on June 15, 1984, at my home church the Wheeler Addition Church of God, presided by Minister Harvey Robinson. It wasn't long before I started to think about children, and reminiscing on the time my chemotherapy doctor informed me that I probably wouldn't be able to have any because of the six months of chemo I had to endure; again I had to trust God, there I was in a marriage and couldn't have children, so I prayed "Lord, do something, I want children, you haven't fail me yet, and I trust that you will bless me still".

Sheila and Anthony's wedding

In December of 1984 I joined my husband in Germany; we were there for eleven months together until we were given orders to return to the States (USA), our assignment was Fort Benning Georgia, which was our home for the next eight years. Initially I told Anthony that I was not going to stay in Fort Benning, because I miss my mom, and I wanted to stay with her for awhile, he said ok, and that he would come up every weekend to see me. I was home for three weeks and I was ready to move back with my husband. We moved into housing and bought our first set of furniture; a living room, dinner set, and china cabinet, it was nice to have something we could call our own.

In January 1986, I discovered that I was pregnant, our first child, yes, another miracle. I prayed that the first child would be a boy, and the doctor told me it was a boy, because of the heart beat (boys had a stronger and faster beat than girls), in fact my family had a baby shower for me and all the gifts was for a boy; at the time of the birth (before I could see the baby), I can recall immediately gazing at Anthony, and I noticed the strange look on his face, along with his exclaim "it's a girl"; yes, Miranda, a big plump ball of joy, was our first child, we loved her and tried to show her to the world. Approximately two years later Anthony II (AJ) our son was born; I got what I wanted, not necessarily in the order I requested, but the Lord knew best and gave them in the order that was needed.

Anthony, Miranda, Sheila, and AJ

In the late 80's while there in Columbus, we found a great church, "Victory drive Church of God", a family oriented, and God centered church. It was a mixed congregation (black and white), with a double barrel preacher as a pastor, yes, a musician and a preacher; brother Avery had that ability to take a soul to a spiritual high with the tickling of the ivory (piano), which complimented his soothing vocals, then afterward, he would bring you back to reality with his toe stumping, fire and brimstone messages. The Church was our extended family, we had many friends there, two of our closes friends were Velma and her husband Terrell Jones. We spent a lot of time together; usually on Saturday mornings, Velma and I would go to garage and yard sales, then afterward we would go out and eat, what a great time we had, she was and still is to this day a spiritual sister and a good friend.

In the spring of 1990, rumors were soaring around the military community that our spouses were going to war, because Sadam Hussan refused to leave Kuwaite. In July of that same year our worse fears became a reality; the only combat brigade (my husband unit) on Fort Benning was going to war, "Wow", I thought, "my husband's going to war, and I'm here with two children, what am I going to do?" After attending my first family support meeting and seeing the other spouses meet and greet one another, I became encouraged to stay strong and support my husband and his fellow soldiers as they deployed to do what they were trained and paid to do. Anthony was sent to war, and was there for nine months, and of the five thousand soldiers from our community that went, less than ten was wounded or killed, that in itself was a blessing, considering the hundreds of service members that didn't make it back, or the thousands that came back wounded physically or psychologically (post traumatic stress disorder). When the soldiers returned, we gave them a welcome home celebration like no one in the area had ever seen before. The surrounding towns were delighted to have the soldier's home as well; I think it was only because they were losing a lot of money without the soldiers patronizing their businesses and the families eating together in restaurants.

In the winter of 93 Anthony departed for his third tour to Germany, The children and I stayed behind because they had about five months of school yet to complete; we did join him that summer, the kids first plane ride, and my second tour to Germany. Initially, I didn't like it, Buamholder Germany was hilly and unexciting to me, but when Anthony took me to the church, I felt at home; it was my first time in a Church of God in Christ (COGIC) service, and "wow" the spirit was really moving. It was amazing, more than 200 people in the service each week and no one was over the age of 40; we had Elders, Ministers, Deacons (Anthony was one), Missionaries, and a older looking woman we call mother wise, she was a good friend, I later found out that I was older than she, but I still respected her because of her Godly wisdom.

On two separate occasions we traveled to Paris France for the weekend, it was really nice. We rode the elevator to the top of the Eiffel Tower; it was beautiful having the opportunity to glance over Paris at night, but I was glad to get back on the ground, because I am dreadfully afraid of heights. We got to see the original painting of the Mona Lisa; I really didn't understand the hoopla surrounding a (estimated size) 25 inch x 17 inch painting, the area they had roped off around it seemed to be about 25 feet x 25 feet, and crowds of people leaned over the ropes to take distance shot pictures of that little painting. Miranda and A.J was with us on both trips to Paris, don't know if they remember any of it, because they were only 8 and 6 years old at the time.

The original painting of Mona Lisa as displayed
in a museum in Paris France

Finally, after the kids started school, I felt that I needed to find a job, so I became FCC (Family Child Care) certified, and began to keep children 2 to 4 years of age in our apartment. I enjoyed that job for two years before I sought employment with the community day-care center; it was only about a five minute walk from our apartment. I was hired and enjoyed being around other adults of the same profession; we shared experiences, and their successes encouraged me to become more educated in the child care field. In the fall of 96 Anthony was told that he was selected to be promoted to Sergeant Major (SGM), which meant he would also have to go to Texas to attend the Academy. We really didn't want to leave Germany; we had many friends, a great church, and a very close happy family, but in June of 97 we departed to begin our eleven month stay in El Paso (Fort Bliss) Texas.

-4-
"A Faithful life in Prosperity"

3 John 1:2 *Beloved, I pray that you may prosper in all things and be in health, just as your soul prospers.*

    Our arrival to El-Paso was a smooth transition; Anthony and the children started school, which left me at home alone, so I worked on a volunteered basis at the local military day care center until I was eventually hired full time. It took us only about three weeks to find a church; we initially went to the Gospel service (combination of Baptist, AME Zion, and Methodist), but we didn't feel welcome, the congregation was large but the people didn't seem sincere when they greeted us. We tried another chapel on post the following week, it was an Apostolic Church of God; there were only about eight people in the congregation and four of them were children, but oh what great a spirit filled service we had. The pastor's wife played the keyboard, Elder Diggs played the drums, and sister Neal ushered and sang with the two musicians as part of the praise team, Anthony and I immediately knew our family were needed there, he joined the praise team and I assisted sister Neal as a usher, while Miranda and AJ joined the other children as part of the congregation.

    I had other friends there at Fort Bliss, whose husbands were in the academy with Anthony, but none was as close as Valeria Neal, we did a lot together; her husband was stationed their, so she knew the area well. El-Paso is in the middle of the desert and across the border from Mexico, so there was a lot to do; when we weren't eating at some buffet, red lobster, or one of the many Mexican restaurants, we were walking through the malls, or crossing the border into Mexico and shopping. Chaplain Robinson (our pastor) and his wife were very nice; Sister Robinson was from the Philippians, and a very good cook, her miniature egg rolls were my favorite. Everyone there at the chapel were of one spirit and very loveable and easy to get along with.

Sheila's baptism at the church in Texas

We were only in Texas for a year, before we were reassigned back to Georgia. One of the few things I didn't like about the military, was as soon as you bond with a person or group it's time to move on, other than that and the possibility of my husband going to war, I loved the lifestyle, it was an endless adventure. We both prayed to get back to Fort Benning Georgia, the birthplace of Miranda and AJ, and the location of my best friend Velma Jones. Anthony had completed his training at the Sergeants Major Academy, and was assigned as the Battalion Sergeant Major for the Officer Candidate School there at Benning; so I called Velma and told her that we were coming back to Georgia.

Anthony and Sheila at a Military ball

In late June of 98 after a two day drive from El-Paso TX. to Tampa FL. and a two week vacation; one in Tampa with Anthony's family, and the other with my Mother in Pikeville. When we did finally arrive into Columbus Georgia, We found Velma's house; it was a large and lovely home, and she welcomed us with opened arms. She asked if we had a place to stay until we were given housing, I replied "no", so she opened her home to us while we waited on housing. Velma had not changed in over six years, which was the last time I saw her, she talks, talks, talks (a lot like my sister charlotte and cousin Diana), and I enjoy her company. We also got to meet the new addition to her family, little Miriam; she was a little cute chubby four year old when we arrived. Velma and her husband Terrell had been praying for twelve years for a child, so I was very happy to see that their prayers were answered. We stayed with Velma and Miriam for two weeks, her husband Terrell had retired from the military and taken on a contracting job in Saudi Arabia; so I, Anthony and the children got to know Velma and Miriam very well. Velma and I spent a lot of time laughing and talking, just as we did six years earlier, catching up on changes and new events.

Miriam Jones

After about two weeks there with Velma and Miriam, we received on post housing; only a five minute walk from Anthony's job, and a three minute walk from A.J's school, Miranda went to school on post as well, but she had to catch the bus at the corner from the house. While Anthony was at work and the children were in school, I spent the first few weeks of our move in unpacking and getting the house in order, of course, I left the heavy stuff for my husband. Shortly after getting housing, I applied for work at one of the three day care centers on post; it took about six months, but I was eventually hired at the Santa Fe center. The Director for the center, Ms Elliott, was a very smart and savvy lady; I enjoyed talking, and learning from her.

-5-
"Faith Regenerated"

James 1:2, 3 My brethren, count it all joy when you fall into various trials, knowing that the testing of your faith produces patience.

One evening in the fall of 99, Anthony was watching television, Miranda and AJ were in their rooms; as I was setting in my pajamas on the side of the bed, debating on which book to read, I was moved to place my hand into my pajama top to feel my left breast. When doing so I discovered a knot, so I jump up (without saying a word) and went to the bathroom, closing the door behind me, because Anthony was in the room. I looked into mirror, and saw the knot, and it was about the size of a quarter, and floated as I guided it with my finger. With confusion and fear running through my head, I went back into the bed room and sat back on the bed; I afraid and didn't tell Anthony what I found. The next morning I called Martin Army Hospital and told my doctor what I had found, so she made me an appointment to come in and see her on the following morning. On the evening after talking to the doctor, I informed Anthony on what I had discovered when he got home that night; neither of us wanted to think the worst, so we didn't talk about it that much. The next day Anthony and the kids hugged me and went off to work and school as normal and I went to my doctor; she inspected the knot and asked me a series of questions, then followed up with a needle biopsy there in her office.

The longest eight days of my life was waiting on the biopsy result; with every passing moment I feared the results, Anthony tried to keep me encourage, we prayed, but we didn't want to alarm anyone else, but I am sure church members suspected something because I stayed on my knees at the alter and constantly asked for prayer. One morning on day eight (since the biopsy) I picked up the phone, fighting within myself, praying and debating on rather I should call the doctor for the results or wait for her nurse to call me. I finally punched in the seven numbers, then whispered my name to the receptionist, and stated the purpose of my call, she then transferred me to my doctor, who picked up the phone, greeted me, then revealed to me, at that time my worst fear; she told me that the results were positive for cancer, and she wanted me to come in to discuss my options, so I did.

When Anthony got home that evening, I told him of the biopsy result and the treatment options the doctor discussed with me; we hugged and cried, then we decided to have the breast removed, which was the more favorable option. Before the breast surgery, the doctor had to remove and test eight lymph-nodes from my left arm pit, to assess at what degree the cancer had spread; fortunately, only one of the eight lymph-nodes were affected with the virus, so my scheduled date of surgery was 2 weeks prier to Thanksgiving. After the lymph-nodes surgery, Anthony and I told Miranda and AJ, I don't know if they really understood the severity of the disease, but I felt that they needed to know; we also informed our pastor and other lay leaders in our church, and of course, my mom, the sweetie who was there from the beginning of it all, I informed her, my siblings, and other family members there in Pikeville. I knew that my body was under attack and I needed all the prayers that I could get to help me fight that battle.

The day prior to my surgery, Minister Thornton, along with her husband and our pastor Chaplain Baker came to visit me at our home; they prayed with me and my family, then afterward we sat and ate the banana pudding I had made earlier. Having them come by was very encouraging. On the day of surgery, Anthony and my friend Velma was their when they prepped and rolled me out and into surgery, at that time I weren't worrying about the breast cancer, because I knew that Jesus had healed me of Hodgkin disease (cancer) more than 15 years earlier, and when the Son set you free, you are free indeed, God don't make mistakes. After having my left breast removed, I awoke and remember seeing my husband Anthony, Velma, both ministers Thornton, and the nurses. One of the nurses asked me if I wanted something to eat, I replied "yes, a T-bone steak, baked potato and a toss salad"; they all laughed at me, but I was serious, the nurse spoke up and said "Mrs. Johnson you can't have that", so she went and got me some jello.

The following morning after surgery they sent me home with two drainage tubes in my side, they were a little restricting, but I got around ok; most of the time Anthony was there to help drain the tubes. About a week after surgery, Anthony took me back to the hospital to have the drainage tubes removed, and oh what a relief it was, I was free to move around as I please. I took thirty days off from work, then resumed working at the child developmental center throughout my 6-month of chemotherapy, I was not a candidate for radiation. This time around chemo was a breeze; the only time I got sick was on my last treatment. One problem I did encounter after the third month of chemo was a sever memory lost, some of the simplest things I would forget; I would leave the house to go to the mall, and after several minutes of mindless ridding, I would finally remember that I was going to the mall, another incident was when I left work on a one hour lunch break, and returned only to have the lead teacher ask "where have you been?" and I replied "to lunch", she responded by saying, "but you've been gone for two hours". It's a terrible feeling to lose your memory.

After the final chemo treatment, my breast reconstruction surgery was scheduled at emery in Atlanta, the plastic surgeon there inspected the area, and we agreed that with an implant the left chest could be developed into a 34-B; the surgeon also inspected the right breast and determined that it also needed a small implant in order to balance out with the reconstructed left side, ultimately, the surgery was a success. Within about two years after the surgery Lymph edema set in my left arm which prevented me from doing any heavy lifting. From that day on I had to wear a compression sleeve and glove on my left arm. After explaining this to Mrs. Elliotte, at that time the center director, she was very understanding, and transferred me to work with older children that I didn't have to lift, and eventually I was transferred to Georgia Pre-K and worked as an assistant teacher for four and five year olds.

Sheila with her Georgia Pre-K class

On one particular day in 2006 at a hair store, I tripped and landed on my hands, catching all of my body weight with my arms and shoulders. I didn't experience any pain at the time, but about eight hours later while I was at home my left arm started to hurt; the pain was so sever that I couldn't sleep. Anthony got out bed and gave me a pain reliever and some water; I felt a little relief but not much, I twist and turned all through the night because of the discomfort. The following morning I was so tired and sleepy that I couldn't go to church, so Anthony went alone because he had to teach Sunday school. Later that morning I took off my compression sleeve and glove and notice that my arm was as red as a beet; that really did scare me, I remembered my doctor telling me to get to a hospital if my arm ever starts turning red and feels hot, so I drove myself to the ER, because Anthony had gone to Sunday school and A.J. and Miranda were gone to work, when I got their I explained to them my situation, and showed them my arm; they immediately took me to the back and determined that I had an infection, so they started an I.V, and worked hard to keep the infection from moving up the arm. I stayed in the hospital for three days; thank God the infection didn't spread. God has really been good to me!

In 2007 while playing with the pre-K students at work, I stumbled and again caught myself with both hands, I didn't feel hurt; but because of my situation I was directed to go to the ER for insurance purposes. As time went on my shoulders and arms started to give me more problems each passing day. It was bad enough that I couldn't lift more than 10 pounds with the Lymph edema arm; but the right arm eventually started to hurt from the many years of over use. My last day of work was January 29, 2009; I had to take an early retirement because of the stress and pain in my arms shoulders. I was told by the doctors that I'd over used my right arm, and had osteoarthritis in both shoulders. I could no longer do simple household chores; vacuuming, hanging curtains, mopping floors, my daughter had to do it all. In spite of it all, I recognized that God was still good and worthy to be praised!

-6-
"Faith in the Resurrection"

2 Corinthians 5:7, 8. *For we walk by faith not sight. We are confident, yes, well please rather to be absent from the body and to be present with the Lord.*

February 26, 2006 was a very trying time for me; that was the day my mom died. I will never forget that Sunday night I received the call; my baby brother Ray, from Tennessee called me and said "Sheila, momma is really sick; I don't think she is going to make it." I replied "what?" He said "I don't think she's going to make it, I think you should come home." I said "ok I'm on my way," then he told me that they were going to take her to Erlanger hospital in Chattanooga and that he would call me back. I said ok, but I couldn't wait for their call, I ran into our guess bathroom closed the door and I cried out to God "Please! Please! Don't let my mom die please!" I came out of the bathroom went into my closet crying and walking back and forth trying to get some clothes together. The phone rang again this time it was my cousin Diana. I asked "how is momma?" She replied "Sheila." I asked again, "Diana! How is my momma?" then she asked to speak with Anthony; I gave him the phone and I heard Anthony say "Oh no!" I knew then that momma was gone; I cried and cried like I've never cried before.

Monday morning, Anthony and I headed out to Pikeville; usually when I'm headed home, I'm excited, but this time my life was crumbling, I had lost my very best friend, my momma. Many may criticize and remind me that Jesus is our best friend, and I'll tell them that even he cried when he lost his earthly friends, John the Baptist, and Lazarus. The drive to Pikeville is normally a 4 ½ hour trip, but that morning it seemed as though it took twelve hours. As we arrived in to Pikeville, we drove down the drive way toward my mom's house; as we parked I gazed toward the front door, hoping to see my mom's head peeking through the crack of the door to see who was pulling up, that didn't happen. I went inside the house, hugged and greeted family and friends there, then went straight into my momma's room, closed the door, then lay on her bed and cried; words could not explain how I felt. Anthony came in and laid beside me, then told me that he was going to get 3 hours of rest before driving back to Troy, Alabama (which was where he worked as a JORTC instructor); he told me to call and inform him on the date of the funeral, so that he, Miranda and AJ could schedule time off to attend.

On the evening of my day of arrival; me, Charlotte, and the boys (other siblings) went over to the funeral home to pick out our mom's casket. I didn't want to go, but my brothers and sister insisted that I go; after looking for awhile, we finally agreed on the one we all liked. The wake was on Tuesday, and funeral the following day, our mom looked like an angel resting peacefully; I kissed her on the forehead and rubbed her hands; I knew the body was only a shell, but it was nice to see my mom for the last time. The funeral was at our home church, the Wheeler addition Church of God, where Reverend Leola McClain had been the pastor for more than 50 years at the time. The church was packed with friends, family and people only mom knew; she was well known and loved by many, and they did show it, by flooding the funeral home with flowers, and the house with food.

Sheila poses with her mom at an earlier reunion

My mom was the best of all my friends; she was a woman with many talents; a real good cook, an excellent singer, and a decent actress. Mom had a slight hump in her back, and walked with a cane, she had many medical issues; high blood pressure and a bad heart to name a few. It's been a number of years since her death, and it still doesn't seem real. Three years prior to mom's passing, my sister Charlotte had tried to talk to me about her death and place of burial, but I did not want to entertain the thought of that ever happening. About a year later, while sitting in church there in Pikeville, a vision of a casket appeared at the front of the church; and I said to myself, "what is this?" as I continued to envision people walk pass and gazed into the coffin. I then noticed myself peeking into the coffin and seeing my mom laying there peacefully; I cried to myself, "mama I tried my best to get here in time." I believe that was God's way of letting me know that her time to come home was drawing near. Our momma was blessed to have been here for 80 years, and we were truly blessed to have enjoyed her for the many years we did. There were many times when I really wanted to talk, hug, and kiss my mom; but I realize that she can never return to be with me, but I will someday be with her, resting comfortably in the presence of Jesus; where there's no sorrow, nor pain, yes, momma's made whole.

-7-
"Faithfully Encouraged"

Psalm 119:50 *This is my comfort in my affliction, for your word has given me life.*

On the evening of September 15, 2010, after stepping out of the shower and drying off; I noticed a knot on the side of my right breast. I continued to dry off and put on my clothes, anxiously plotting my next decision; realizing that if I called the ER, there would be nothing for them to do except inform me to wait and contact my personal physician; so I did, and after a sleepless night, I called the hospital and asked the receptionist if I could see my primary doctor that day. The receptionist checked Dr. Gray's calendar and told me that she had no opening until the following week; so I explained to her my situation and told her that I couldn't wait, and then she proceeded to tell me that a Dr. Adams was free to see me at 3 pm. While waiting for my appointment, I ate lunch, prayed, and listened to some **healing CD's** while combing my hair. After arriving to see Dr. Adams, I explained to her about the knot I'd found on the side of my breast. She went through the normal procedure in asking questions about the date and results of my last mammogram; she did a biopsy of the knot, then sent it off to be evaluated, and told me it would take about two weeks for the results.

AJ, Miranda, Anthony, and Sheila

I initially didn't tell my husband, even when he asked why I'd gone to the hospital, I told him it was nothing to worry about; it may have been the wrong thing to do, considering he has stood by me in all situations like this before. I did tell Anthony after the biopsy, and we agreed to pray and expect the results to be negative; but they came back positive, so I called and informed all my prayer warrior partners from the past; My friend Velma, who has always been there when I needed her, and Evangelist Thornton, who placed a healing seed in my life three days prior to me finding the mass in my breast; it was when Velma and I greeted the evangelist after church, and Velma told her about the many medical problems she had, the evangelist then told us of the healing CD's that she had in her car to give us, and those are the CD's I'd been listening to every night and morning prior to the knot discovery; never did it enter my mine that I would be diagnosed with cancer again, but God knew what he was getting me ready for. I called my pastors from back home; sister McClain, who reminded me of what God had already done, and encouraged me to keep the faith; then I talked with pastor Hollinsworth, who prayed with me over the phone, and stated that when he's witnessing to others concerning faith, he constantly tells them of my testimony, and we agreed that God would do it again.

After being told the results of the biopsy, my personal physician scheduled Anthony and I an appointment to discuss surgery and other options with a general surgeon; so we met with Dr. Brasswell, who asked questions about the implant that was placed in my healthy right breast ten years earlier; I think his concern was possibly damaging the chest muscle in order to get the cancerous mass. Then he explained that he would also be removing several lymph-nods from my right arm pit, and pending there biopsy results, that will determine what degree of radiation or chemo that will be needed; as he was talking, he did not realize that Anthony and I had already talked about me definitely not taking the radiation, and possibly looking for an alternative to the poisonous chemotherapy; we had decided to trust God and his miraculous healing power. The surgery was scheduled for the following Thursday, October 7.

When we went to church Sunday, I went up to the alter for prayer, and evangelist Boggin walked up to me and told me that the Lord told her to pray for me; so we prayed and prayed as I thanked God for my healing. I told my friend Velma that I received my blessing with a healing at the same time; and when I got back to my seat I shouted for a good five minutes, thanking the Lord for what he'd done. Before the start of church service, I felt as though the weight of the world was on my shoulder, I couldn't stop crying; but before the end of service, oh what a relief, all fear was gone, I felt great.

On the day of the surgery, I had to be there by 10am; so Anthony took a week off from work to be with me. We got there and I changed into my rob, Anthony and I waited for about thirty minutes before the doctor entered and told Anthony that he was taking me to pre surgery; so Anthony kissed me and left the room. For the next seven hours I was out of it; When I did come through, in a semi-conscious state, I noticed Anthony, Velma, and evangelist Boggin staring and smiling; I couldn't really make out the words they were saying, but it seemed pleasing, so I smiled. When I did awake fully, the only face there were Anthony; he told me that the other guest had left because they saw that I was tired. He then told me that after the surgery, the doctor came out and told him and sister Jones that the tumor had attached itself to the implant (I had it installed in 99) instead of the wall of my body, which was a good sign; and he went on to tell them that he had to cut very little of the chest muscle, which was also good; "what a mighty God we serve", when I sat and think about it all, I just laugh and cry out "thank you Jesus for another miracle."

During the course of my two day recovery in the hospital, many friends and church members came to see me, Pam Edward and sister Odom was the first to come into the room, then Velma and Simon walked in about five minutes later; we all talked, laugh and praised God, as Velma explained the exciting information given to her and Anthony by the doctor the previous day. About 30 minutes into our praise session, Miranda walked in through the door (she was on her two hour lunch break), she greeted every one then silently listened to the conversations. I could sense that it was getting a little crowded in the room, especially after Anthony told me that he had to go and get three more chairs from the conference room so that every one could have a seat; shortly afterward, sister Pam and Odom gave me a hug then told me they had to leave, "it was really great seeing sister Pam". Simon then stated, "let me do what I came here for", as she reached into a plastic bag and pulled out a bottle of anointing oil, then she and Velma begin anointing and praying over me; it was very refreshing, my first post surgery anointing; we then talked a little more, and then they two had to leave. Sister Anderson, a member of the usher board came by with some beautiful flowers; she stayed for about an hour, finally, the day ended, just as it started, with Anthony and me, the only two left in the room.

I was released from the hospital around noon on Saturday morning, and I was so happy to get home. Anthony had two days left on his personal leave days; so he took care of the measuring and cleansing of the three drainage tubes attached to my side, it had to be measured and cleaned every eight hours. Miranda and AJ helped me out when Anthony wasn't present; he ensured they knew what they were doing. Many of my in-laws and church friends called to check on me the day after surgery, and I thanked them for their prayers and concerns. Anthony went to church on Sunday, because he had to teach Sunday school; he told me that many people asked about me and expressed their love and prayers; I really do believe that the prayers of the saints and the mercies of God are the power that's keeping me. On that Monday, Anthony's final day from work, Pastor Scott (a former chaplain in charge of our Gospel service) called and asks if he and his wife could come over to visit, and I replied, "Yes", I'm always available for a minister of God to visit. They came over for about an hour, and we prayed and talked. Anthony had informed me earlier that he had come by to visit while I was in surgery at the hospital; it is so good to know that so many people love you.

I went back for my follow-up on Thursday, hoping to get the drainage tubes out, and praying for a good report from the result of the lymph-node test; well, the doctor did remove the tubes, however, the lymph-nodes result hadn't gotten back yet, so he told me to call back on the following week. On Monday morning I called the clinic, requesting to speak with Dr. Brasswell, they patched me through and he begin to explain, "Ms Johnson, I have some good news," I got so excited I couldn't wait for the rest of his statement, but I kept my silence and listened; he went on to explain that of the 12 lymph-nodes removed, there were no trace of cancer in any. "What a Mighty God we serve," that very aggressiveness tumor wrapped itself around my implant, instead of sticking to the wall of my body, therefore, it didn't invade my body; I immediately called Anthony, then Velma, and it seemed like everybody else in the world to tell them about the good news. Yes, Another Miracle, Performed by God!!!

My prayer is for everyone who reads this book to get something out of it. I did not write it to attain sympathy; but to encourage those who have gone through, or know someone who has gone through similar trials. This is my testimony; for God is an unfailing God, he will do just what he says. "If the Lord doesn't do anything else for me, he has already done enough! May God richly strengthen and bless every person who reads my story.